CW0881444

CLOUDY DAYS ARE SUNNY TO ME

Cloudy Days Are Sunny To Me

Dana Alberson

Copyright © 2021 by Dana Alberson.

Library of Congress Control Number:		2021901318
ISBN:	Hardcover	978-1-6641-5357-8
	Softcover	978-1-6641-5356-1
	eBook	978-1-6641-5355-4

All rights reserved. No part of this book may be reproduced or transmitted
in any form or by any means, electronic or mechanical, including photocopying,
recording, or by any information storage and retrieval system,
without permission in writing from the copyright owner.

The views expressed in this work are solely those of the author and do not
necessarily reflect the views of the publisher, and the publisher hereby disclaims
any responsibility for them.

Any people depicted in stock imagery provided by Getty Images are models,
and such images are being used for illustrative purposes only.
Certain stock imagery © Getty Images.

Print information available on the last page.

Rev. date: 01/20/2021

To order additional copies of this book, contact:
Xlibris
844-714-8691
www.Xlibris.com
Orders@Xlibris.com
822279

CONTENTS

Dedication

To my Daddy, there is no greater love.

In Appreciation

I will take advantage of this moment, for surely no better time like the present may be afforded me to say a word than now.

In this opportunity, I glance backward to the first time I set eyes on you.

That introduction was a celebratory occasion for me as it definitely changed the entire course of my life. Anxiously was I in search of purpose and true happiness, and grateful was I to find such pure source of inspiration in such a good friend, to him whom I have the deepest love of all . . . to him I am thankful.

Dana A. Alberson

To my daughters whom I love with all my heart. It's never been easy and I apologize for that. I have always wanted nothing but the best for you. I pray every day that you understand the struggle, the choices, the decisions I made along the way and that all of my shortcomings made you into stronger women—you have your own sky to fly . . . there is no limit.

Love,

Mama

Cloudy Days are Sunny to Me is inspired by a true friend, she always has an ear to hear when we get together she inspired me along the way with her words and acts of kindness. Thank you Linda Thigpen and family

Cloudy Days Are Sunny to Me was inspired by a true friend. The title of this book was inspired by the landscape and scenery in Hawaii while visiting EWA Beach and by the healing power of loving life and learning that love and truth will set you free. Positive thinking got me to this point. I'm trying to imagine what other great things can happen.

INTRODUCTION

Why does the ocean make me cry. I sniveled as I walked down the tan sandy beach, I thought of how many times the water rolled up against me; and as quickly as it came, it left. How many times, I thought, I saw a pretty seashell only to go reach for it and the tide would tease me by taking it back. How many times was I fortunate to spot one, quick enough to get ahold of it, admire it for its beauty, and cry as I thanked the ocean for sharing such a beautiful part of its love. The ocean loved me and I loved it back.

The power of positive thinking is almost unbelievable but I know it to be true. We are the creators of our own lives, captains sailing our own ships, masters of our own universe. I have decided after many years that I have my own sky to fly, and I am going to do whatever it takes, for the takeoff begins with me.

Fear, like an imaginary creature in our minds, often keeps us from our dreams, goals, and aspirations. We are afraid of failing, afraid that others will know you fell flat on your face; but I'm here to tell you, that is a monster you should smother, cut up into little bitty pieces, and imagine them blowing off in the wind, never to come back again. Fear has no place in our lives—it is useless.

I grew up in a dysfunctional home, but where lots of love was present. I attended an old fashion Southern Baptist church where prayer could make you or break you. God was bigger than anything in the sky and that if you prayed hard enough, he would answer you. As the years went by and my curiosity was enlightened, it is now my belief that "God" is not a man in a box standing behind the clouds. God is an energy that we will never be able to explain mathematically, scientifically, or otherwise; and it is my belief that the energy that wakes us up, the sunshine, the clouds to appear, and the ocean to roll back and forth, is the same energy that can cause our creative juices to start flowing and make our dreams, goals, and aspirations to come into fruition.

The thoughts and expressions which follow here are manifestations; seeds being sown and conversations with myself. Every woman needs to express her essence at some point in time. It is my desire that my thoughts will lead you to an undiscovered talent and that you will find comfort there. Love yourself. Live your life. Always listen to your small/big inner voice and say, "I am . . ." and fill in the blanks.

Cloudy Days Are
Sunny to Me

The sun came up as it always does—so bright I can hardly see it up there in the sky; it is my destiny.

I love to feel the sun dance across my shiny little face. When it kisses me so much my cheeks become rosy; it caresses me but others hide amongst the shade—*heat, warmth, hot waves.*

To see golden beams peer out between the clouds is such a heavenly sight; something you will never see at night.

While the sun can bring such heatwaves, it is the clouds that I crave to shield me from that illustrious light. Shape-shifting mind-lifting evaporated particles of light high above set the sun so bright. Even behind the clouds, the sun shines illuminating reflections to create bows of color. As I look to the heavens, I will always see those cloudy days are sunny to me.

Take the mask off! You're hiding all that beauty!

Go without makeup, it's so refreshing.

Drink a glass of water.

Get some fresh air.

Close your eyes and breathe.

*

Don't get mad when you are asked a question. A question is to obtain information that one is interested in—being nosy, inquisitive, curious, misunderstood. Be glad they are interested in you!

On this page, write your own poem or write a goal you want to reach. Write whatever you want but always come back to it!

_____

_____

_____

_____

_____

_____

_____

_____

_____

_____

_____

_____

_____

_____

_____

_____

_____

_____

To take a risk one operates in the Law of Action. You can only achieve that thing which you desire by acting on it; just as the pen that I used to write these words: I had to pick it up, forcibly write my thoughts down. The pen can't write on its own!

Start that paperwork you've been meaning to fill out.

Make a vision board.

Act upon your thoughts. It can take you wherever you want to go. No ifs or buts—just do it.

It's OK if you fail or fall flat on your face. You can still use the Law of Action to get up! Start all over again!

Not All Men Are Bad, Just Misunderstood Fulfillment in the Future

I think a good man wants happiness and fulfillment in his future.

He can be incapable in many ways and compatible in other small ways. It's up to each individual what he can and cannot deal with. A "bad" man is out for his own self-gratification and from whatever pain he has endured in his life. Perhaps he has not come to a point yet when he is willing to deal with it; hence, he loves no one and he doesn't care about the future.

A "good" man is out to show gratitude to others; and from whatever pains he has endured, he makes sure no one else ever has to feel that kind of pain again.

He looks to the future.

Men are trained to believe that money equals power, and that power is a path to respect. However, power and control in a relationship are not compatible with intimacy.

Relationships succeed only when both partners are willing to display their insecurities and vulnerabilities to each other. It's important for men to know that failing to share power cheats them out of the intimacy and love they want.

All men want to be loved.

It's Raining Again

Mother Nature is at it again, but tonight she is vicious: pounding away against the roof of my celestial heart. But what some would find so destructive, I find much joy in the sounds of the beatings she brings. Tears turn into rays of light which soon fall into the night; melodies and tunes that have been heard before reach deep down into my core. I will position myself and seek refuge under the canopy of your strength. I find it is soothing like a mantra, this sacred utterance you bring. It makes my heart flutter and dance; there is always another chance to feel this good just like I knew it would.

One of the military tactics is to tear the terrain up with a forced concentration in several areas in which contact has already visualized recon on the land needed to be invaded that mind needs to be reprogrammed!

*

My mind doesn't work like yours; when I'm thinking forward, you're thinking backward.

My downs are your ups. It shouldn't be that way.

My crooked is your straight.

My 7 is your 8.

You should be the encouraging one to say, "Keep going, that's great!"

In this new day and age, there is a conspiracy against mastery. I have continually been bombarded with promises of immediate gratification, instant success, and quick and fast relief—all of which are completely wrong. I had forgotten it myself even as I preach it to others. "Be patient and wait," is a most valuable lesson in life—it is the first lesson!

STARTER KIT TO GROW WILD FLOWERS

Germinate the seedlings indoors in a sunny location, six weeks prior to warm weather. Seeds can be sown directly into the garden when the soil is warm.

No Shade Required

The flowers that I offer from this precious earth are much to be desired, one of a kind. A precious portion of my garden you will love, you will tend to me dig and hoe, unearth scents of springtime. Honeysuckle and rose seeds are needed to multiply the life of this garden year-round, not just for tiny plants but for moistening the ground as well. I will always offer up litter offerings for the care that you will give. Weeds have no place here so that I can live.

You are just within reach of all you ever dreamed of.

Don't give up!

*

Look at yourself in the mirror and tell yourself,

"I want to know you and I want to love you!"

*

Yes, living alone can be liberating. You have freedoms that some would give up anything for, but it is an isolated liberty when you have no one to share a laugh or a cry with.

Find someone of substance.

Because it has no leaves, it doesn't give up its water through evaporation as easily as other plants. Its stems are thick with a lot of room for storing water and have a protective covering that keeps the stored water inside. Some cactus species can go up to two years without water.

I AM CLEARLY NOT A CACTUS.

Oh, but I am like a rose, and a rose should be diligently watered, but please don't drown me. Give me plenty of room to expand and grow, but you must prune me and pay me some attention. Oh, I have thorns I failed to mention.

SISTER SISTAR

Oh, have you ever heard a sister say I am in the AREME? I'm sure you have, if you are still on your journey, we have been the topic of discussions at some point in time. Did you guide her, direct her, or help her find her way? Did you offer her warm words of encouragement on a cloudy day?

Were you an infinite beam of light, a blazing star to follow? Or were you a pill that was so bitter she could not swallow? You had seven days in a week, seven colors to create white light. Do Re Mi Fa So La Ti Do. Does your sister/sistar know how much you love her by the love that you show?

These synchronicities keep happening to me. It will not stop till I'm where I need to be. I have been quickened and awakened by the cold hard truth, I will never ever get back the days of my youth. I will, however, persevere through the truth that I AM the way, the truth, and the light; wish I may wish I might, these vibrations I give and receive will soon make way for a new sight!

I was blinded by your light I could barely see. I became mesmerized by your beautiful dark brown eyes; they have seen so much yet they are brand new. I have dreams of places for you to go and things for you to do.

*

We create as we speak. We are creators of creation.

*

It's time for you to receive your share.

*

I am a benefit to all I come in contact with, never a liability.

Contradictions and Inconsistencies

Did we come from nothing or did we come from clay? Contradictions it seems are the topic of life per se. Six or eight, so we will say seven. We will even throw in, there's a place called heaven.

I have been forsaken, no I have not. These inconsistencies will forever be a block. Think with your own mind and with your own heart. Man will never know the ending or know how to start. Too busy to find out on your own; no book will save us from becoming bones. We were born and we will die, and in between life will pass you by. Live, love, laugh, is what they say. Fight for freedom, justice, and the great being you way. Do kind and generous gestures; love with a big heart. The energy we could create is the catalyst you may to an everlasting, infinite eternity. Eternity like you and me has always been and it shall always be.

CURSIVE WRITING

To some, it can be complicated to read.

I am a woman who has curves like the letters of cursive writing. Every line is defined, connecting each one to another. So eloquently designed; every t crossed and all the i's dotted.

Around each winding curve, you would tend to get lost from the top of my head to the soles of my feet like perfect penmanship so precise, so neat. I promise if you take the time to read me closely and read every fine line, you will get a clear message every single time.

NULL AND VOID

Just like the title, you are redundant and have no validity with me anymore. You failed to function as you should; everything you do is so cliché. If you were not a man, I would think you were gay. With misery and despair, you have become the source of great distress. So I dismiss you, get this stress off my chest.

*

Hope for a man who can turn stress into streams of joy.

Men Are Hunters, Women Are Gatherers

I want to be elusive enough to keep the hunter hunting but be accessible enough for him not to quit.

A treasure hunter will always keep diving deeper and deeper till he finds what he is looking for.

You are a treasure and someone is hunting for you.

Death or Bust

From me to you . . .

Death rings the bell like an unwanted guest; you have no idea when he will appear. Have you cleaned the house today? Well, he can show up but I will not be at home, and he will have to catch me, I refuse to make it safely to destination Death Valley. I will live dangerously on the edge. I will pick up a stranger to get him farther down the road. I will speed down the highway with the wind blowing in my hair. I welcome a game of Truth or Dare. Red hair I don't care! Live your life the way you want to live. Make indelible memories that permeate your soul. I say go ahead lose control—laugh, cry, scream if you must. I'm holding my sign up saying, "Death or Bust!"

This is a good time. This one moment can change everything you ever did; it can change your future. Stop doing what you have done in the past. Be a master of your present moment! Enjoy!

*

Clouds . . . they constantly undergo change just like people!

*

I might have a headache, so I will take aspirin just in case! Always be prepared.

*

Who's right and who's wrong? Who said so?

I have many scars on me, visible and invisible. They are little notes to remind me of how special I am. I made it. I survived. I cannot be destroyed. I'm not arrogant. I'm not vain. I am not stuck up. I love life—to hell with them. Get to know me and you will be one of the privileged. If you've ever been injured, you remember the pain and how bad it hurt. You can still feel it, can't you? But you survived! I have the biggest smile on my face most days because I am. I am alive!

WEALTH, ADVANTAGE, LUST, OR LOVE YOU GOT WITH THEM FOR ONE OF THE ABOVE

If it was for wealth, did you help them get rich?

Was it advantage and now you have forgotten who they are?

If it was lust, did you value them in any other kind of way?

Was it love and now your heart breaks day by day?

Make sure your motives are true!

Fires bring about destruction, but they also bring new growth. You destroyed something that had to be destroyed in order for me to begin to grow again.

Fires started with a spark and now have brought forth comfort, warmth, and light. You are my fire on the coldest of nights.

*

There is only one me and that's your me; and the me I display in public is more reserved, more tame than the me you get who has no restraints, no reservations. I am all yours!

The Colored Bridge

Beams of light . . . We are but beams of light, prisms bouncing off one another. It is never dark in my world, you see, because you are the light that always seems to guide me. One after the other, I see you every day. You there, sir, with your smile so bright. Hey, lady, you too with them braids so tight . . . Yes, even you on the corner with that beer in your hand. That woman at the edge, wishing she had a good man. As we bounce off one another, our images seem to show. The only difference is some just don't know as we light up, we reflect in different directions but come back to one another—we are all each other's reflections.

Before and After

Can't change the past, can't predict the future. Must float on the rivers of the aftermath. These rains pour so they flood the very ground I stand. Will my feet ever be able to be upon dry land? I must wade, paddle, swim if I want to live and see another day . . . someway, somehow!

Don't give up!

I'm authentic. I have a low tolerance for entanglements, but I am deeply committed to a relationship. I can adapt to our friendship; remain steadfast. I will tell you when you are wrong and praise you when you're right. I can enjoy you, but I also can have a good time without you.

The ground that shakes underneath my feet, the power of one clap of thunder, this rain that falls from a dark sky often make me wonder the energy that flows to and fro, north, south, east, and west. It's so much power for one to digest, but we are the one that makes the earth quake. We will echo through the minds of the ones that know us. We will make you realize we all have a destiny. We are a force to reckon with like a bolt of lightning, bouncing across the midnight sky . . . we will never die.

Mental agitation gets the best of us at some point in time. Emotions are supposed to be a natural intuition. We cannot control everything, but we can control and govern ourselves, and for some that is difficult. Always learning the wiser I get.

*

A rude awakening will show up on you at any point in time. Accept, acknowledge, and accelerate past that point, so that now you can say you had an enlightening experience, a teachable moment, a lesson well learned.

*

A person who is overly concerned with themselves and their material things has no room to value you, much less themselves.

I Am

A beautiful flower was displayed proudly at first on the dining room table. Days go by with no water, you left me lonely for many days to dissipate and wither away.

Don't pick flowers if all you're going to do is let them die.

I am an angel and a devil in the same package. I have a halo and horns. I can be heaven or I can be hell. I'm sugar and spice and everything nice— that's what a real woman is made of.

*

My worst truth and my best lie was that I fell in love with you, but I said I didn't care.

*

I can't promise to fix all of your problems, but I can promise you, you will never be alone.

This thing I have for you is permanent; no medication can cure you from me. I try to eat well, but there is no support group for being addicted to you. My heartbeat accelerates at the thought of you. One fix, two fixes, will never be enough. I want to remember you. Just as alcohol burns as it goes down your throat, my soul burns for you. I am addicted to you. I need you I want you in a daily dose. I am hooked.

CAGED BIRD

Been a caged bird for a while now. Reckon will you ever open the gate for me to be free; and you might as well do for you never enjoy me. I sing to you songs from my heart, yet you never look my direction. I come close to the edge but never get any affection. What's the purpose for you even having me? So you can brag, tell others, "I got this bird, you see"? If you don't let me out, I will become songs of silence—my singing will cease.

You have seen me naked, you have seen me vulnerable, vulnerable to being open. The wounds of my life—it is my greatest asset to be transparent. I hold nothing back; no lies depart from the pearly gates or from my lips. It may be X-rated but always clearly stated. Being vulnerable has also shown me pleasure in fears I once had, of experiences longed for.

Don't Wake Me Up

Knock, knock, knock as I am awoken out of my sleep. It is you . . .
your smile knocking at my eye gates the window to my soul. I am aroused
this morning at your image standing before me like a mirage. I am enticed
to do what I know best, but I will abstain and place myself back to rest.

*

When you strike your match against this phosphorus strip of mine,
you will get a flame every time . . . a flame that brings forth so much fire.
Keep striking that match . . . it will get higher and higher.

Phosphorus Venus Morning Star
Bearer of the Light

That glass you were holding earlier, I am jealous of it. I wish your lips had been sipping on me. I wish your hand was embracing me.

I am an original gal with original ideas. I'm eccentric, you know, you doubt my words and the way I flow, but I can assure you I'm one of a kind—a woman like me is hard to find. I am rare and a good thing, this I know. Please be my friend and never my foe.

I must remove myself from these negative energies; they are draining on my cranium and crumbling to my knees.

Good riddance, goodbye once and for all. It's my turn to kick the ball. I will kick, I will run, I will pass home plate. I will never let your negativity determine my fate.

*

Here at the Alberson School (but you can fill in the blank).

We have a long history of turning out leaders with a formula that works. At Alberson, we believe that academic excellence, career preparation, and civic engagement lead to success. Service matters.

Salt and Sugar

Upon observation, they are alike. If mixed together, you cannot tell the difference in appearance. Upon tasting, there is a clear distinction between the two.

Men are the same.

You can put them side by side. Upon observation, they just look like any other man, but the composition of them may be quite different. A man is needed to spice up a woman's life. Which one will you choose? Salty and sweet, either choice will leave an impact on you sooner or later.

A Window

The wall I stared at for so long never moved. I never had a glimpse outside whether it was sunny or dark, but it was always dark inside the four corners of my mind—boxed in, never to see what was on the other side. Then you came along and started renovations. Without even knowing, you placed a window of happiness on one wall then you placed another full of sunshine. Pretty soon, I could see out of every side. Have I lost my mind? Never again will I ever occupy a space with no windows. It's just not the thing for me. Let there be light, let me be free.

Keep your windows clean.

A Lesson in Arithmetic

We have been taught that Math is exact, its interpretation is disputed as to when and where it was first operated. But one thing I know about mathematics is it has brought value to my life. It has

+ added to my happiness,

- subtracted from my sadness,

and

x multiplied my abilities.

It's not very complicated; it's very elementary. It is a classic method for the solutions to all my problems.

=

Equal

I am distinguished from any animal, yet I act like one—I lose control at the thought of you who captured my heart, like a creature in the forest who's been caught in a metal trap. I can still have a chance to escape. Is it worth the fight or do I enjoy this unmerciful pain that has entrapped me? I do. Does that mean something is wrong with me?

SAINTS AND SINNERS

On a website I was browsing, a picture popped up of a group of strippers praying.

Many people had something negative to say while others had a positive outlook on this image.

Biblically most of Jesus's followers were murderers, liars, and thieves. Oh, and don't forget Jesus supposedly shacked up with a prostitute. At least they were trying to do something positive, that is, if they were attempting to pray. Who can and cannot pray? Is there a particular kind of person who should pray? Saints and sinners . . . we all want the same thing.

You should look at everyone as if they were a book. What is interesting, if any, about them? What is your favorite chapter or have you ever gotten to know them, to read them?

What do you anticipate to happen in the end?

I Am a Rose with Thorns

Love is like thorns in a rose. You really don't feel its piercing embellishments till you attempt to touch the rose. The rose is frail but you also see its strength. It is guarded by those thorns that can bring so much pain, but were there to protect the rose because its petals are soft and gentle, yet strong enough to withstand strong winds.

A man that carries a handkerchief may have been waiting all his life to show one that lending it to her is the last act of chivalry.

My father still carries a handkerchief; he is eighty-six.

*

You are not here to make someone happy.

You are here to enhance their happiness.

I surrender, submit, succumb to this feeling I have. They say love is blind but I beg to differ. Love is enlightening; it is colorful, vibrant, and warm. It is the calm before the storm. Love for some could be heart aching; for me, it has given me purpose yet painstaking. When I close my eyes, my senses, even in my subconscious, are aware that I would give anything just to be there in the arms of the one who cares, in the aroma of love as found in the most fragrant flowers, and to see a friendly luminescent smile. I don't want to hear just a little while longer, I need love now and forevermore. Oh, how I wish you would enter through my door. Love for me comes naturally; it is not forced even in the worst circumstances. I can see it at a glance. The energy it takes to love can be death-defying, awe-inspiring, or can be poetry in motion and filled with such devotion. Tears running down the cheek of the one you love can swell your heart that it's too much to take . . .

Love can be calming, but by the same token, it can cause calamities the likes you've never seen! Wars have been started and are never-ending for such a love so deeply felt. It reverberates like lightning, striking on the stormiest night. *I cannot live without it!*

*

Disappointment is not the story you want to tell!

*

There are many gems and precious stones across the world's continents. Some are so dangerous to obtain that many lose their lives in pursuit of this wealth. Some that seek are rewarded with their discovery, but those that conclude that the earth has not revealed her finest beauty . . . I am the most precious gem of all!

My idea of daydreaming is alone time well spent on a trip not taken yet with the one who distracts you from the hustle and bustle of everyday stresses.

Daydreaming can put your mind at ease, like the sunshine warming your skin on a beautiful spring day and other days. It's a real tease.

This image I see is like a mirage in the desert; I see an oasis!

Say It with Me: in the Mirror!

You are successful, desirable, and I admire your confidence. I don't like you 'cause you're winning; I like you because I know you are able to make a comeback. You are not a loser and you will never give up. I believe in you.

I love you.

Just as a bird needs both its wings to fly, I need both of you—can't have one without the other. I am so glad that both of you chose me as your mother. I am the happiest when the two of you are near—your laughter, your silliness, your funny little cheer. You have made taking flight fearless and free. You have made me over time want to soar above the trees looking down. I know I have wings and no longer bound. I take sole ownership of the truth. I am nothing without you.

Race . . . is supposed to be a competition amongst runners. Who is the fastest to complete a set course and achieving an objective? It is not about your skin color . . . Can you tell the color of a man by his skeleton? The kidneys or lungs out of the body cannot tell you the color of the individual that housed those organs. The race right now that seems to attract everyone is who can die an ugly death because if you do not have love in your heart and peace within your mind, you are headed toward a sad destruction.

Get to know the man in the corner.

Shake your neighbor's hand.

Ask your coworker to lunch.

The shackles that you say enslave me are no longer . . . but you have now made me crumble. At least I tried to hold my head up with dignity and stay humble, and yet I am ashamed I fell flat on my face, covered with the dust of the soles of the past. The French, Irish, and African alike, forced or at will, I never had a choice . . . to really be free. Now as I lay here on this cold hard ground, who will tend to me? Will you still hold it against me that they changed me? This is not the real me, I am still LADY LIBERTY! I was given to you as a gift now looked upon as a curse. You changed the way I look, you took away the children that I nursed—my true beauty. It is your birthright and duty . . . in whomever you trust to defend for the people, the good and the just . . .for your loved ones no matter the color of the skin, dark or fair, long locks or straight hair. Unless you plan on leaving the fight if you dare . . .

I want to believe that one day, I will rise with the beauty that I see in everyone's eyes, the tears that have been shed, the battles that we tread. We will fight together—black, white, yellow, brown, and red. We are people. Stay united, not divided.

God Allah Buddha   Power in numbers

Train yourself to keep that which you fear to have! Don't be afraid to be rich. Don't be afraid to have a beautiful life. Don't be afraid to dream. Don't be afraid to lose. Don't be afraid to have it all!

*

Though I may appear to be simple, I am the most complex being you will never be able to figure out! I am relevant, I am intelligent! I AM AN EARTHling!

ENERGIZED VIBRATIONS

Lightning Source UK Ltd.
Milton Keynes UK
UKHW012334050221
378341UK00009B/447/J

9 781664 153578